Born in 1960

by

Kerry Butters.

Born in 1960.

Millennium: 2nd millennium

Centuries: 19th century – **20th century** – 21st century

Decades: 1930s 1940s 1950s – **1960s** – 1970s 1980s 1990s

Years: 1957 1958 1959 – **1960** – 1961 1962 1963

1960 (MCMLX) was a leap year starting on Friday (dominical letter CB) of the Gregorian calendar, the 1960th year of the Common Era (CE) and *Anno Domini* (AD) designations, the 960th year of the 2nd millennium, the 60th year of the 20th century, and the 1st year of the 1960s decade. It is also known as the "Year of Africa" because of major events—particularly the independence of seventeen African nations—that focused global attention on the continent and intensified feelings of Pan-Africanism.

Contents

Events

January

- January – The state of emergency is lifted in Kenya, officially ending the Mau Mau Uprising.
- January 1 – Cameroon gains its independence from French-administered U.N. trusteeship.
- January 2 – U.S. Senator John F. Kennedy (D-MA) announces his candidacy for the Democratic presidential nomination.
- January 6 – The Associations Law comes into force in Iraq, allowing registration of political parties.
- January 9–11 – Aswan High Dam construction begins in Egypt.
- January 10 – British Prime Minister Harold Macmillan makes the Wind of Change speech for the first time (see February 3).
- January 14 – The Reserve Bank and Commonwealth Bank are created in Australia.
- January 15 – The first televised anime, *Three Tales*, debuts on NHK.

- January 19 – The Treaty of Mutual Cooperation and Security between the United States and Japan is signed in Washington, D.C.
- January 21 – A coal mine collapses at Coalbrook, South Africa, killing 435 miners.
- January 22
    - In France, President Charles de Gaulle fires Jacques Massu, the commander-in-chief of the French troops in Algeria.
    - Jacques Piccard and Don Walsh descend into the Mariana Trench in the *bathyscaphe Trieste*, reaching the depth of 10,911 meters (35,797 feet) and become the first human beings to reach the lowest spot on Earth.
- January 24 – A major insurrection occurs in Algiers against French colonial policy.
- January 25 – In Washington, D.C., the National Association of Broadcasters reacts to the payola scandal by threatening fines for any disc jockeys who accepted money for playing particular records.
- January 28 – The National Football League announces expansion teams for Dallas to start in the 1960 NFL season, and Minneapolis–St. Paul for the 1961 NFL season.
- January 30 – The African National Party is founded in Chad, through the merger of traditionalist parties.

February

- February 1 – In Greensboro, North Carolina, four black students from North Carolina Agricultural and Technical State University begin a sit-in at a segregated Woolworth's lunch counter. Although they are refused service, they are allowed to stay at the counter. The event triggers many similar non-violent protests throughout the Southern United States, and six months later the original four protesters are served lunch at the same counter.

A section of lunch counter from the Greensboro, North Carolina Woolworth's where the Greensboro sit-ins began is now preserved in the Smithsonian Institution National Museum of American History

- February 3 – Prime Minister of the United Kingdom Harold Macmillan makes the Wind of Change speech to the South African Parliament in Cape Town (although he had first made the speech, to little publicity, in Accra, Gold Coast — now Ghana — on January 10).
- February 5 – The first CERN particle accelerator becomes operational in Geneva, Switzerland.
- February 9
    - Joanne Woodward receives the first star on the Hollywood Walk of Fame.
    - Adolph Coors III, the chairman of the board of the Coors Brewing Company, is kidnapped, and his captors demand a ransom of $500,000. Coors is later

found murdered, and Joseph Corbett, Jr. is indicted for the crime.
- February 10 – A conference about the proposed independence of the Belgian Congo begins in Brussels, Belgium.
- February 11
    - The N-class blimp *ZPG-3W* of the U.S. Navy is destroyed during a storm over Massachusetts.
    - Twelve Indian soldiers die in clashes with Red Chinese troops along their small common border.
- February 13 – France tests its first atomic bomb in the Sahara Desert of Algeria.
- February 18 – The 1960 Winter Olympics begin at the Squaw Valley Ski Resort, in Placer County, California.
- February 26 – A New York-bound Alitalia airliner crashes into a cemetery at Shannon, Ireland, shortly after takeoff, killing 34 of the 52 persons on board.
- February 29 – The 5.7 Mw Agadir earthquake shakes coastal Morocco with a maximum perceived intensity of X (*Extreme*), destroying Agadir, and leaving 12,000 dead and another 12,000 injured.

March

The iconic picture of Che Guevara."

- March 2 – Lucille Ball files for divorce from husband Desi Arnaz after 19 years of marriage. The divorce ends the *I Love Lucy* franchise.
- March 3 – Elvis Presley returns home from Germany, after being away on military duty for 2 years.
- March 5
  - Elvis Presley receives his honorable discharge from the U.S. Army.
  - Alberto Korda takes his iconic photograph of Che Guevara, *Guerrillero Heroico*, in Havana.
- March 6
  - Vietnam War: The United States announces that 3,500 American soldiers will be sent to Vietnam.
  - The Canton of Geneva in Switzerland gives women the right to vote.

- March 17 – Northwest Orient Airlines Flight 710 crashes near Tell City, Indiana, killing all 63 on board.
- March 21 – The Sharpeville massacre in South Africa results in more than 69 dead, 300 injured.
    - Ayrton Senna – Brazilian racing driver who won three Formula One world championships in 1988, 1990 and 1991 is Born: March 21, 1960, São Paulo, São Paulo, Brazil
- March 22 – Arthur Leonard Schawlow and Charles Hard Townes receive the first patent for a laser.
- March 23 – Soviet premier Nikita Khrushchev meets French president Charles de Gaulle in Paris.
- March 29 – "Tom Pillibi" by Jacqueline Boyer (music by André Popp, text by Pierre Cour) wins the Eurovision Song Contest 1960 for France.

April

Tiros I prototype on display at the Smithsonian National Air and Space Museum

- April 1
    - Tuanku Abdul Rahman ibni Almarhum Tuanku Muhammad, 1st Yang di-Pertuan Agong of Malaysia,

dies in office. He is replaced by Hisamuddin Alam Shah ibni Almarhum Sultan Alaeddin Sulaiman Shah, Sultan of Selangor.
- The United States launches the first weather satellite, TIROS-1.
- The 1960 United States Census begins. There are 179,323,175 U.S. residents on this day. All people from Latin America are listed as white, including blacks from the Dominican Republic, European whites from Argentina and Mexicans who resemble Native Americans.

- April 4
  - At the 32nd Academy Awards ceremony, *Ben-Hur* wins a record number of Oscars, including Best Picture.
  - Elvis Presley's song "Are You Lonesome Tonight?" is recorded for the first time.
- April 9 – Gunman David Pratt shoots South African Prime Minister Hendrik Verwoerd in Johannesburg, wounding him seriously.
- April 12 – Eric Peugeot, the youngest son of the founder of the Peugeot Corporation, is kidnapped in Paris. Then, he is released on April 15 in exchange for $300,000 in ransom.
- April 13
  - United States launches navigation satellite Transit I-b.
  - The proposed mass-production of the Blue Streak missile is cancelled.
- April 19 – April Revolution: South Korean students hold a nationwide pro-democracy protest against President Syngman Rhee, eventually leading him to resign from that office.

- April 21 – In Brazil, the country's capital (Federal District) is relocated from the city of Rio de Janeiro to the new city, Brasília, in the highlands. The actual city of Rio de Janeiro becomes the State of Guanabara.
- April 27 – Togo gains independence from France, with the French-administered United Nations Trust Territory being terminated.

May

Francis Gary Powers wearing special pressure suit for stratospheric flying

- May 1
  - Several Soviet surface-to-air missiles shoot down an American Lockheed U-2 spy plane. Its pilot, Francis Gary Powers of the Central Intelligence Agency, is captured.
  - In India, May 2 is declared as 'Maharashtra Divas', i.e., Maharashtra Day (also celebrated as 'Kaamgaar Divas', i.e., Workers Day).

- May 3
  - The European Free Trade Association (EFTA) is established.
  - *The Fantasticks*, the world's longest-running musical, opens at New York City's Sullivan Street Playhouse, where it will play for 42 years.
- May 4
  - West German refugee minister Theodor Oberländer is fired because of his past with Nazi Germany.
  - A. J. Liebling promulgates Liebling's Law in *The New Yorker* magazine: "Freedom of the press is guaranteed only to those who own one."
- May 6 – United States President Dwight D. Eisenhower signs the Civil Rights Act of 1960 into law.
- May 9 – The U.S. Food and Drug Administration announces that it will approve birth control as an additional indication for Searle's Enovid, making it the world's first approved oral contraceptive pill.
- May 10 – The U.S. nuclear-powered submarine USS *Triton*, under the command of Captain Edward L. Beach Jr., completes the first underwater circumnavigation of the Earth (codenamed Operation Sandblast).
- May 11 – In Buenos Aires, four Mossad agents abduct the fugitive Nazi criminal against humanity, Adolf Eichmann, in order that he can be taken to Israel and put on trial. (Eichmann is later convicted and executed).
- May 13 – A joint Swiss and Austrian expedition makes the first ascent of the Asian mountain, Dhaulagiri, the world's 7th highest mountain.

- May 14 – The Kenyan African National Congress Party is founded in Kenya, when 3 political parties join forces.
- May 15 – The satellite Sputnik 4 is launched into orbit by the Soviet Union.
- May 16
  - Soviet premier Nikita Khrushchev demands an apology from President Dwight D. Eisenhower for the U-2 reconnaissance plane flights over the Soviet Union, thus aborting the summit meeting scheduled for Paris in 1960.
  - Theodore Maiman operates the first laser.
- May 18 – Real Madrid beats Eintracht Frankfurt 7-3 at Hampden Park, Glasgow and wins the 1959–60 European Cup (football).
- May 20 – In Japan, police carry away socialist members of the Diet of Japan. The Diet next approves a mutual security treaty with the United States.
- May 22 – The Great Chilean earthquake: Chile's subduction fault ruptures from Talcahuano to Taitao Peninsula, causing the most powerful earthquake on record (with a magnitude of 9.5) and a tsunami. Because of its power, the seismographs in the city of Valdivia are overloaded and malfunction through the entire earthquake.
- May 23 – Prime Minister of Israel David Ben-Gurion announces that Nazi war criminal Adolf Eichmann has been captured.
- May 27 – In Turkey, a bloodless military coup d'état removes President Celâl Bayar and installs General Cemal Gürsel the as head of state.

- May 30 – Cemal Gürsel forms the new government of Turkey (its 24th government, composed mostly of so-called "technocrats").

June

- June 1 – New Zealand's first television station begins broadcasting in the city of Auckland.
- June 5 – The Lake Bodom murders occur in Finland.
- June 7 – U.S. Senator John F. Kennedy wins the California Democratic primary.
- June 9 – Typhoon Mary kills 1,600 people in China.
- June 10 – Domino's Pizza is founded.
- June 15
  - Violent demonstrations at Tokyo University result in 182 arrests, 589 injuries.
  - The BC Ferries company, later to become the second-largest ferry operator in the world, commences service between Tsawwassen and Swartz Bay, British Columbia, Canada.
- June 19 – The Associated Broadcasting Company (now TV5) is founded in the Philippines.
- June 20 – The short-lived Mali Federation, consisting of the Sudanese Republic (now the Republic of Mali) and Senegal, gains independence from France.
- June 23 – Japanese prime minister Nobusuke Kishi announces his resignation.
- June 24 – Joseph Kasa-Vubu is elected as the first President of the independent Congo.
- June 26

- The State of Somaliland (the former British Somaliland protectorate) receives its independence from the United Kingdom. Five days later, it unites as scheduled with the Trust Territory of Somalia (the former Italian Somaliland) to form the Somali Republic.
- The Malagasy Republic, now Madagascar, becomes independent from France.
- June 30
  - The Belgian Congo receives its independence from Belgium as the Republic of the Congo (Léopoldville). A civil war follows closely on the heels of this.
  - Public demonstrations by democratic and left forces, against Italian government support of the post-fascist Italian Social Movement, are heavily suppressed by police.

July

- July 1
  - Ghana becomes a republic and Kwame Nkrumah becomes its first President.
  - Cold War: A Soviet Air Force MiG-19 fighter plane flying north of Murmansk, Russia, over the Barents Sea shoots down a six-man RB-47 Stratojet reconnaissance plane of the U.S. Air Force. Four of the U.S. Air Force officers are killed, and the two survivors are held prisoner in the Soviet Union.
  - The Trust Territory of Somaliland (the former Italian Somaliland) gains its independence from Italy. Concurrently, it unites as scheduled with the five-day-

old State of Somaliland (the former British Somaliland) to form the Somali Republic.

- July 4 – Following the admission of the State of Hawaii as the 50th state in August 1959, the new 50-star Flag of the United States is first officially flown over Philadelphia.
- July 10 – The Soviet Union national football team defeats the Yugoslavian national football team 2–1 in Paris to win the first European Soccer Championship.
- July 11
  - Congo Crisis: Moise Tshombe declares the Congolese province of Katanga independent. He requests and receives help from Belgium.
  - Harper Lee publishes her novel *To Kill a Mockingbird*, which later wins the Pulitzer Prize for the best American novel of 1960.
- July 12 – Chin Peng is exiled from Malaysia to Thailand and the Malayan state of emergency is lifted.
- July 13 – U.S. Senator John F. Kennedy is nominated for President of the United States at the 1960 Democratic National Convention in Los Angeles.
- July 14 – The United Nations Security Council decides to send troops to Katanga to oversee the withdrawal of Belgian troops.
- July 20 – Ceylon elects Mrs. Sirimavo Bandaranaike as its Prime Minister, the world's first elected female head of government. She takes office the following day.
- July 21 – Francis Chichester, English navigator and yachtsman, arrives at New York City aboard his yacht, *Gypsy Moth II*, crossing the Atlantic Ocean solo in a new record of just forty days.

- July 25 – The Woolworth Company's lunch counter in Greensboro, North Carolina, the location of a sit-in that had sparked demonstrations by Negroes across the Southern United States, serves a meal to its first black customer.
- July 25–July 28 – In Chicago, the 1960 Republican National Convention nominates Vice President Richard Nixon as its candidate for President of the United States, and Henry Cabot Lodge Jr., as its candidate to become the new Vice-President.

August

- August 1 – Dahomey, now known as Benin, becomes independent from France.
- August 3 – Niger becomes independent from France.
- August 5 – Upper Volta, now known as Burkina Faso, becomes independent from France.
- August 6
  - Cuban Revolution: In response to a United States embargo against Cuba, Fidel Castro nationalizes all American and foreign-owned property in Cuba.
  - In the Republic of the Congo (Léopoldville), now the Democratic Republic of the Congo, Albert Kalonji declares the independence of the "Autonomous State of South Kasai".
- August 7 – The Ivory Coast becomes independent from France.
- August 7 – The world's first standard gauge passenger preserved railway, The Bluebell Railway, opens to the public.

- August 11 – Chad becomes independent from France.
- August 13 – Ubangi-Shari becomes independent from France, as the "Central African Republic". It later becomes the "Central African Empire" for some years.
- August 15 – Middle Congo becomes independent from France, as Republic of Congo (Congo-Brazzaville).
- August 16
  - Joseph Kittinger parachutes from a balloon over New Mexico at an altitude of about 102,800 feet (31,333 meters). Kittinger sets world records for: high-altitude jump; free-fall by falling 16.0 miles (25.7 kilometers) before opening his parachute; and the fastest speed attained by a human being without mechanical or chemical assistance, about 982 k.p.h (614 m.p.h.). (Kittinger survives more or less uninjured, and he is still alive in Florida as of 2013. Felix Baumgartner breaks his record in 2012.)
  - The Mediterranean island of Cyprus receives its independence from the United Kingdom.
- August 17
  - The newly named Beatles begin a 48-night residency at the Indra club in Hamburg, West Germany.
  - Gabon becomes independent from France.
  - The trial of the American U-2 pilot Francis Gary Powers begins in Moscow.
- August 19
  - Cold War: In Moscow, American U-2 pilot Francis Gary Powers is sentenced to 10 years in prison for espionage.
  - Sputnik program: The Soviet Union launches the satellite Sputnik 5, with the dogs Belka and Strelka (the

Russian for "Squirrel" and "Little Arrow"), 40 mice, two rats and a variety of plants. This satellite returns to earth the next day and all animals are recovered safely.
- August 20 – Senegal breaks away from the Mali Federation, declaring its independence.
- August 25
  - The 1960 Summer Olympic Games begin in Rome.
  - The American nuclear submarine USS *Seadragon* surfaces through the Arctic ice cap at the North Pole, the first submarine ever to do so.
- August 29 – Hurricane Donna kills 50 people in Florida and New England.

September

- September 1
  - Sultan Hisamuddin Alam Shah, Sultan of Selangor and 2nd Yang di-Pertuan Agong of Malaysia, dies in office. He is replaced by Tuanku Syed Putra, Raja of Perlis.
  - Disgruntled railroad workers effectively halt operations of the Pennsylvania Railroad, marking the first shutdown in the company's history (the event lasts two days).
- September 2 – The first elections of the Parliament of the Central Tibetan Administration are held. The Tibetan community observes this date as Democracy Day.
- September 5
  - 1960 Summer Olympic Games: Muhammad Ali (then Cassius Clay) wins the gold medal in light-heavyweight boxing.

- The Congolese president, Joseph Kasa-Vubu, fires Patrice Lumumba's entire government, and also places Lumumba under house arrest.
- September 6 – William Hamilton Martin and Bernon F. Mitchell, two American cryptologists, announce their defection to the Soviet Union at a press conference in Moscow.
- September 8 – In Huntsville, Alabama, U.S. President Dwight D. Eisenhower formally dedicates the Marshall Space Flight Center (which had been activated by NASA on July 1).
- September 14
  - Colonel Joseph Mobutu takes power in Republic of the Congo via a military coup.
  - The countries of Iran, Iraq, Kuwait, Saudi Arabia, and Venezuela form OPEC.
- September 22 – Mali, the sole remaining member of the "Mali Federation" following the withdrawal of Senegal one month earlier, declares its full independence as the *Republic of Mali*.
- September 26 – The leading candidates for President of the United States, Richard Nixon and John F. Kennedy, make the first televised debate.
- September 30 – The television animated sitcom, *The Flintstones* premiers on ABC.

October

- October 1
  - Nigeria becomes independent from United Kingdom, and Nnamdi Azikiwe becomes its first native-born Governor General.
  - Cameroon declares independence from United Kingdom.
- October 3 – Jânio Quadros is elected President of Brazil for a five-year term.
- October 5 – White South Africans vote to make the country a republic.
- October 7 – Nigeria becomes the 99th member of the United Nations.
- October 12
  - Cold War: Soviet premier Nikita Khrushchev pounds his shoe on a table at a meeting of the United Nations General Assembly, his way of protesting the discussion of the Soviet Union's policies toward Eastern Europe.
  - Inejiro Asanuma, chairman of the Japan Socialist Party, is assassinated by Otoya Yamaguchi using a *wakizashi* (samurai sword) during a political debate in Tokyo being taped for broadcast on Japanese television.
- October 13
  - The third John F. Kennedy – Richard M. Nixon Presidential Debate takes place.
  - The Pittsburgh Pirates defeat the New York Yankees in the seventh game of the World Series on Bill Mazeroski's series-clinching home run.
- October 14

- Presidential candidate John F. Kennedy first suggests the idea for the Peace Corps of the United States.
- The Premier of New South Wales officially opens Warragamba Dam, one of the world's largest domestic water supply dams.
- October 24 – Nedelin catastrophe: A large rocket explodes on the launch pad at the Baikonur Cosmodrome, killing at least 90 people of the Soviet space program.
- October 26 – Robert F. Kennedy telephones Coretta Scott King, the wife of Dr. Martin Luther King Jr., and secures King's release from jail regarding a traffic violation in Atlanta.
- October 29 – In Louisville, Kentucky, Cassius Clay (later Muhammad Ali) wins his first professional boxing match.
- October 30 – Dr. Michael Woodruff carries out the first successful kidney transplant in the United Kingdom, at the Edinburgh Royal Infirmary.

November

November 15: Polaris missile test

- November 2 – Penguin Books is found not guilty of obscenity, in the case of D. H. Lawrence's novel *Lady Chatterley's Lover*.
- November 8 – United States presidential election, 1960: In a close race, Democratic U. S. Senator John F. Kennedy is elected over Republican U. S. Vice President Richard Nixon, to become (at 43) the second youngest man to serve as President of the United States, and the youngest man elected to this position.
- November 13 – Sammy Davis Jr., marries Swedish actress May Britt.
- November 14
  - Belgium threatens to leave the United Nations over criticism of its policy concerning the Republic of the Congo.
  - A collision between two trains in Pardubice, Czechoslovakia, kills 117 people.
- November 15 – A Polaris missile is test-launched from Cape Canaveral, Florida
- November 22 – The United Nations supports the government of Joseph Kasavubu and Joseph Mobutu in the Republic of the Congo.
- November 24 – The professional basketball player Wilt Chamberlain of the Philadelphia 76ers gets 55 rebounds in an NBA game versus the Boston Celtics.
- November 28 – Mauritania becomes independent of France.

December

- December
  - The African and Malagasy Organisation for Economic Cooperation (OAMCE) (Organisation Africain et Malagache de Coopération Économique) is established.
  - Édith Piaf's recording of "Non, je ne regrette rien" is released in France.
- December 1
  - Patrice Lumumba, deposed premier of the Republic of the Congo, is arrested by the troops of Colonel Joseph Mobutu.
  - A Soviet satellite containing live animals and plants is launched into orbit. Due to a malfunction it burns up during re-entry.
- December 2
  - The Archbishop of Canterbury, the Most Rev. Geoffrey Francis Fisher, talks with Pope John XXIII for about one hour in Vatican City. This is the first time that any chief of the Anglican Church had ever visited the Pope.
  - U.S. President Dwight D. Eisenhower authorizes the use of $1.0 million for the relief and resettlement of Cuban refugees, who had been arriving in Florida at the rate of about 1,000 per week.
- December 4 – The admission of Mauritania to the United Nations is vetoed by the Soviet Union.
- December 5
  - Pierre Lagaillarde, who led the insurrections in 1958 and 1960 in Algeria, fails to appear in court in Paris,

France. He had reportedly fled with his four fellow defendants to Spain *en route* to Algeria.
- ○ *Boynton v. Virginia*: The Supreme Court of the United States declares that segregation in public transportation is illegal in the United States.
- December 7 – The United Nations Security Council is called into session by the Soviet Union in order to consider Soviet demands for the Security Council to seek the immediate release of former Congolese Premier Patrice Lumumba.
- December 8 – For the first time, Mary Martin's *Peter Pan* is presented as a stand-alone two-hour special on NBC instead of as part of an anthology series. This version, rather than being presented live, is shown on videotape, enabling NBC to repeat it as often as they wish without having to restage it. Although nearly all of the adult actors repeat their original Broadway roles, all of the original children have, ironically, outgrown their roles and are replaced by new actors.
- December 9
  - ○ French President Charles de Gaulle's visit to Algeria is bloodied by European and Muslim rioters in Algeria's largest cities. These riots cause 127 deaths.
  - ○ The classic British TV series *Coronation Street* premieres. Planned as a 13-part drama, it becomes such a success among viewers it continues to be shown five times per week through 2012.
- December 11 – MGM's *The Wizard of Oz* is rerun on CBS only a year after its previous telecast, thus beginning the tradition of annual telecasts of the film.
- December 12 – The Supreme Court of the United States upholds a lower Federal Court ruling that the State of

Louisiana's racial segregation laws are unconstitutional, and overturns them.

- December 13
  - 1960 Ethiopian coup attempt: While Emperor Haile Selassie of Ethiopia visits Brazil, his Kebur Zabagna (Imperial Bodyguard) leads a military coup against his rule, proclaiming that the emperor's son, Crown Prince Asfaw Wossen Taffari, is the new emperor.
  - The countries of El Salvador, Guatemala, Honduras, and Nicaragua announce the formation of the Central American Common Market.
  - The U.S. Navy's Commander Leroy Heath (pilot) and Lieutenant Larry Monroe (bombardier/navigator) establish a world flight-altitude record of 91,450 feet (27,874 m), with payload, in an A-5 Vigilante bomber carrying 1,000 kg (2,200 lb), and better the previous world record by over four miles (6 km).
- December 14
  - Antoine Gizenga proclaims in the Democratic Republic of the Congo that he has taken over as the country's premier.
  - First tied Test by the West Indian cricket team in Australia in Brisbane.
- December 15
  - King Mahendra of Nepal deposes the democratic government in his country and takes direct control himself.
  - King Baudouin of Belgium marries Doña Fabiola de Mora y Aragón.
- December 16

- Secretary of State Christian Herter announces that the United States will commit five nuclear submarines and eighty Polaris missiles to the defense of the NATO countries by the end of 1963.
- New York mid-air collision: A United Airlines DC-8 collides in mid-air with a TWA Lockheed Constellation over Staten Island in New York City. All 128 passengers and crewmembers on the two airliners, and six people on the ground, are killed.

- December 17 – Troops loyal to Emperor Haile Selassie in Ethiopia overcome the coup that began on December 13, returning the reins to the Emperor upon his return from a trip to Brazil. The Emperor absolves his own son of any guilt.
- December 19 – Fire sweeps through the USS *Constellation*, to become the U.S. Navy's largest aircraft carrier, while she is under construction at the Brooklyn Navy Yard; killing 50 workers and injuring 150.
- December 27 – France sets off its third A-bomb test at its nuclear weapons testing range near Reggane, Algeria.
- December 31 – Last day on which the farthing, a coin first minted in England in the 13th century, is legal tender in the United Kingdom.

Date unknown

- The American Football League is established as a rival league to the NFL.

World population

- World population: 3,021,475,001
    - Africa: 277,398,000
    - Asia: 1,701,336,000
    - Europe: 604,401,000
    - Latin America: 218,300,000
    - North America: 204,152,000
    - Oceania: 15,888,000

Births

January

Michael Stipe

Nigella Lawson

Mohammad Javad Zarif

- January 2 – Naoki Urasawa, Japanese manga author and artist
- January 4
  - Art Paul Schlosser, American comedian,singer and songwriter
  - Michael Stipe, American rock singer (R.E.M.)
  - April Winchell, American writer and voice actress
- January 6
  - Kari Jalonen, Finnish ice hockey player
  - Howie Long, American football player
  - Nigella Lawson, English journalist, broadcaster, television personality, gourmet, and food writer
  - Miriam O'Callaghan, Irish media personality
- January 7 – Mohammad Javad Zarif, Iranian politician, diplomat
- January 10
  - Negro Casas, Mexican professional wrestler
  - Brian Cowen, Taoiseach of Ireland
  - Samira Said, Moroccan singer
- January 12
  - Oliver Platt, Canadian actor
  - Dominique Wilkins, American basketball player

- January 13 – Kevin Anderson, American actor
- January 18 – Mark Rylance, English actor, theatre director and playwright
- January 20 – Will Wright, American computer game designer
- January 21
    - Toxey Haas, American entrepreneur, founder of Haas Outdoors, Inc.
    - Mamoru Nagano, Japanese designer
- January 22 – Michael Hutchence, Australian rock musician (INXS) (d. 1997)
- January 23 – Patrick de Gayardon, French skydiver and skysurfing pioneer (d. 1998)
- January 24
    - Rick Leventhal, American news journalist
    - Mária Bajzek Lukács, Hungarian Slovene writer, adjunct of the University ELTE
- January 26 – Charlie Gillingham, American keyboardist
- January 28 – Robert von Dassanowsky, American cultural historian, writer and producer
- January 29
    - Gia Carangi, American model (d. 1986)
    - Sean Kerly, British field hockey player
    - Greg Louganis, American diver
- January 30 – Alex Titomirov, Russian-American businessman

February

Robert Smigel

James Spader

Prince Andrew, Duke of York

Naruhito

- February 2 – Jari Porttila, Finnish sports journalist
- February 3
    - Marty Jannetty, American professional wrestler
    - Joachim Löw, German football manager
    - Kerry Von Erich, American professional wrestler (d. 1993)
- February 7
    - Yasunori Matsumoto, Japanese voice actor
    - Robert Smigel, American actor, comedian, and puppeteer
    - James Spader, American actor
- February 8
    - Benigno Aquino III, 15th President of the Philippines
    - Alfred Gusenbauer, Chancellor of Austria
- February 9 – Frederik Ndoci, Albanian singer, songwriter, poet, writer, actor and international Recording artist
- February 13
    - Pierluigi Collina, Italian football (soccer) referee
    - Gary Patterson, American football coach
- February 14 – Jim Kelly, American football player
- February 16 – Cherie Chung, Hong Kong actress

- February 18
    - Gazebo, Italian musician
    - Tony Anselmo, American animator and voice actor
- February 19 – Prince Andrew, Duke of York, British prince and second son of Elizabeth II and The Duke of Edinburgh
- February 20
    - Wendee Lee, American voice actress
    - Kee Marcello, Swedish rock guitarist (Easy Action, Europe)
- February 21
    - Henry G. Brinton, American writer and minister
    - Laurent Petitguillaume, French radio and television host
- February 23 – Naruhito, Crown Prince of Japan
- February 27 – Andrés Gómez, Ecuadorian tennis player
- February 28
    - Tōru Ōkawa, Japanese voice actor
    - Dorothy Stratten, Canadian model and actress (d. 1980)
- February 29 – Richard Ramirez, American serial killer (d. 2013)

March

Adam Clayton

- March 2
  - Hector Calma, Filipino basketball player
  - Debra McMichael, American professional wrestling valet
- March 4
  - Mikko Kuustonen, Finnish singer and songwriter
  - John Mugabi, Ugandan boxer and World Junior Middleweight champion
- March 7
  - Joe Carter, American baseball player
  - Ivan Lendl, Czech tennis player
- March 8
  - Finn Carter, American actress
  - Jeffrey Eugenides, American author
- March 10 – Anne MacKenzie, Scottish broadcaster
- March 12 – Minoru Niihara, Japanese singer (Loudness)
- March 13
  - Adam Clayton, Irish rock bassist (U2)
  - Joe Ranft, American animator (d. 2005)
- March 14 – Kirby Puckett, American baseball player (d. 2006)
- March 16 – Jenny Eclair, British comedian, actress and novelist
- March 18 – Richard Biggs, American actor (d. 2004)
- March 19 – Simo Aalto, Finnish magician
- March 20
  - Roxanne Kernohan, Canadian actress (d. 1993)
  - Norm Magnusson, American artist
- March 21
  - Ayrton Senna, Brazilian race car driver (d. 1994)

- Robert Sweet, American rock drummer (Stryper)
- March 23 – Nicol Stephen, Scottish politician
- March 24
  - Kelly Le Brock, American model and actress
  - Annabella Sciorra, Italian-American actress
  - Jan Berglin, Swedish cartoonist
  - Nena, German singer
- March 26 – Marcus Allen, American football player
- March 27
  - Hans Pflügler, German footballer
  - Renato Russo, Brazilian singer (Legião Urbana) (d. 1996)
- March 29 – Hiromi Tsuru, Japanese voice actress

April

Hugo Weaving

Brad Garrett

J. Christopher Stevens

- April 1 – Michael Praed, British actor
- April 2 – Linford Christie, British athlete
- April 3 – Elizabeth Gracen, American beauty queen, actress and model
- April 4 – Hugo Weaving, Australian actor
- April 10 – Fabio Golfetti, Brazilian musician and record producer (Violeta de Outono, Gong)
- April 11 – Jeremy Clarkson, English journalist and television show host
- April 13 – Rudi Völler, German footballer and manager
- April 14 – Brad Garrett, American actor, comedian and voice actor
- April 14 – Myoma Myint Kywe, Burmese Writer and Historian
- April 15 – Susanne Bier, Danish film director
- April 16
  - Wahab Akbar, Filipino politician (d. 2007)
  - Rafael Benítez, Spanish football manager
  - Pierre Littbarski, German footballer and coach
- April 18
  - Neo Rauch, German painter

- o J. Christopher Stevens, American diplomat, U.S. Ambassador to Libya (d. 2012)
- April 19 – Frank Viola, American baseball player
- April 20 – John Altenburgh, American blues and jazz musician
- April 22 – Tatiana Thumbtzen, American actress, model and dancer
- April 23
  - o Valerie Bertinelli, American actress
  - o Steve Clark, English guitarist (Def Leppard) (d. 1991)
  - o David Gedge, English musician (The Wedding Present and Cinerama)
  - o Léo Jaime, Brazilian writer, actor and musician (João Penca e Seus Miquinhos Amestrados)
  - o Claude Julien, Canadian ice hockey coach
  - o Craig Sheffer, American actor
- April 25 – Michael Lohan, American television personality; father of Lindsay Lohan
- April 28
  - o Steven Blum, American voice actor
  - o John Cerutti, American baseball player and announcer (d. 2004)
  - o Ian Rankin, Scottish crime novelist

May

Gjorge Ivanov

Bono

- May 2
  - Gjorge Ivanov, President of Macedonia
  - Stephen Daldry, English film director
- May 3 – Amy Steel, American film actress
- May 4
  - Andrew Denton, Australian television presenter and comedian
  - Werner Faymann, Chancellor of Austria
- May 6 – John Flansburgh, American singer-songwriter
- May 7 – Adam Bernstein, American music video/television director
- May 8 – Eric Brittingham, American rock bassist

- May 9 – Tony Gwynn, American baseball player (d. 2014)
- May 10 – Bono, Irish rock singer (U2)
- May 14
  - Ronan Tynan, Irish tenor
  - "Dr. Death" Steve Williams, American professional wrestler (d. 2009)
- May 15 – Julian Jarrold, English film and television director and producer
- May 16 – Landon Deireragea, Nauruan politician
- May 17 – John Payne, British voice actor
- May 18
  - Jari Kurri, Finnish hockey player
  - Yannick Noah, French tennis player
- May 19 – Yazz, British pop singer
- May 20
  - John Billingsley, American actor
  - Tony Goldwyn, American actor, voice actor, and film director
- May 21 – Jeffrey Dahmer, American serial killer (d. 1994)
- May 22 – Hideaki Anno, Japanese director
- May 23 – Linden Ashby, American actor
- May 24
  - Guy Fletcher, British keyboardist (Dire Straits)
  - Kristin Scott Thomas, English actress
- May 25 – Amy Klobuchar, American politician
- May 26 – Rob Murphy, American baseball player
- May 29
  - Thomas Baumer, Swiss economist, interculturalist and personality assessor
  - Neil Crone, Canadian actor

- May 31
  - Greg Adams, Canadian ice hockey player
  - Chris Elliott, American actor and comedian

June

Kyle Petty

Thomas Haden Church

- June – Lindsey Coulson, English television actress
- June 2 – Kyle Petty, former NASCAR driver and current sports commentator
- June 4
  - Paul Taylor, American musician (Winger)
  - Bradley Walsh, English actor and comedian
- June 6 – Steve Vai, American guitarist
- June 8

- ○ Diane Meredith Belcher, American concert organist, teacher, and church musician
- ○ Mick Hucknall, English rock singer and songwriter (Simply Red)
- ○ Garth Smith, American pianist
- June 12 – Corynne Charby, French model, actress and singer
- June 14 – Peter Mitchell, Australian newsreader
- June 16 – Peter Sterling, Australian rugby player
- June 17 – Thomas Haden Church, American actor
- June 21 – Kevin Harlan, American sports announcer
- June 22 – Erin Brockovich, American environmental activist
- June 28 – John Elway, American football player
- June 30
  - ○ Angela Raiola, American television personality (d. 2016)
  - ○ Tony Bellotto, Brazilian guitarist and writer

July

Jane Lynch

- July 1 – Kōji Ishii, Japanese voice actor
- July 3
  - ○ Vince Clarke, British musician and composer (Depeche Mode, Erasure)

- o Perrine Pelen, French alpine skier
- July 4
  - o Sid Eudy, American professional wrestler
  - o Barry Windham, American professional wrestler
- July 5 – Pruitt Taylor Vince, American actor
- July 7 – Kevin A. Ford, American astronaut
- July 8 – Thilo Martinho, German composer and singer-songwriter
- July 9 – Charles Gavin, Brazilian drummer and producer
- July 13 – Ian Hislop, British journalist and broadcaster
- July 14
  - o Kyle Gass, American music singer-songwriter-guitarist/actor
  - o Jane Lynch, American actress
- July 15 – Kim Alexis, American model and actress
- July 17
  - o Robin Shou, Hong Kong actor
  - o Jan Wouters, Dutch football player and manager
- July 18 – Anne-Marie Johnson, American actress
- July 19
  - o Atom Egoyan, Armenian-Canadian film maker
  - o Terrie Hall, American anti-smoking and tobacco advocate
- July 21
  - o Ezequiel Viñao, Argentine-born composer
  - o Fritz Walter, German footballer
- July 28 – Harald Lesch, German physicist, astronomer, natural philosopher, author, television presenter, professor of physics
- July 30 – Richard Linklater, American director

- July 31 – Dale Hunter, Canadian ice hockey player and coach

August

José Luis Rodríguez Zapatero

David Duchovny

Antonio Banderas

Sean Penn

- August 1 – Chuck D, African-American rapper (Public Enemy)
- August 4
  - Dean Malenko, American professional wrestler
  - José Luis Rodríguez Zapatero, Prime Minister of Spain
- August 7 – David Duchovny, American actor
- August 8 – Ulrich Maly, German politician and Mayor of Nuremberg
- August 10
  - Antonio Banderas, Spanish actor
  - Kenny Perry, American golfer
- August 12 – Laurent Fignon, French road bicycle racer (d. 2010)
- August 13
  - Koji Kondo, Japanese composer
  - Phil Taylor, English darts player
- August 14 – Sarah Brightman, English soprano singer and actress
- August 16
  - Timothy Hutton, American actor
  - Martha Moxley, American murder victim (d. 1975)
- August 17 – Sean Penn, American actor

- August 19 – Morten Andersen, American football player
- August 23 – Chris Potter, Canadian actor and musician
- August 24 – Cal Ripken Jr., American baseball player
- August 26
    - Branford Marsalis, African-American musician
    - Ola Ray, American actress and model
- August 30 – Chalino Sánchez, Mexican musician (d. 1992)

September

Hugh Grant

Colin Firth

Melissa Leo

- September 1 – Joseph Williams, American singer and film score composer
- September 2 – John S. Hall, American poet and spoken-word artist
- September 4
  - Kim Thayil, American rock guitarist (Soundgarden)
  - Damon Wayans, African-American actor and comedian
- September 5 – Karita Mattila, Finnish soprano
- September 6 – Bob Stoops, American football coach
- September 7 – Phillip Rhee, American actor, producer and writer
- September 9
  - Mario Batali, American chef and host
  - Hugh Grant, English actor and activist
- September 10 – Colin Firth, English actor
- September 11 – Annie Gosfield, American composer
- September 12 – Evan Jenkins, American politician
- September 13 – Kevin Carter, South African photojournalist (d. 1994)
- September 14
  - Melissa Leo, American actress
  - Callum Keith Rennie, Canadian actor
- September 16
  - John Franco, American baseball player
  - Yianna Katsoulos, French singer
- September 17 – Kevin Clash, American actor and puppeteer
- September 19 – Yolanda Saldívar, American murderer of tejano singer Selena
- September 21 – David James Elliott, Canadian actor
- September 22 – Scott Baio, American actor

- September 28 – Jennifer Rush, American singer
- September 29 – Alan McGee, British music industry mogul and musician
- September 30 – Blanche Lincoln, American politician

October

Jean-Claude Van Damme

Diego Maradona

- October 4
  - Ana Patricia Botín, Spanish banker
  - Billy Hatcher, American baseball player
- October 5 – Antônio de Oliveira Filho, Brazilian footballer
- October 6 – Richard Jobson, Scottish rock singer-songwriter, filmmaker, and television presenter (Skids)
- October 7 – Kyosuke Himuro, Japanese singer

- October 9 – Maddie Blaustein, American voice actress (d. 2008)
- October 12 – Alexei Kudrin, Russian Minister of Finance
- October 13 – Joey Belladonna, American heavy metal singer (Anthrax)
- October 17 – Guy Henry, English actor
- October 18
  - Alex Ferrer, Cuban-American television personality, lawyer, and retired judge who presided as the arbiter on *Judge Alex*
  - Jean-Claude Van Damme, Belgian actor
- October 19
  - Kerry Sanders, American news correspondent
  - Jeremy Swift, English television actor
- October 24
  - Jaime Garzón, Colombian journalist and comedian (d. 1999)
  - BD Wong, American actor
- October 26 – Jouke de Vries, Dutch–Frisian politician
- October 28 – Landon Curt Noll, American astronomer, cryptographer, and mathematician
- October 29
  - Finola Hughes, British actress
  - Dieter Nuhr, German comedian
- October 30 – Diego Maradona, Argentine footballer
- October 31 – Reza Pahlavi, Crown Prince of Iran

November

Tilda Swinton

Stanley Tucci

Jonathan Ross

Yulia Tymoshenko

- November 1 – Tim Cook, current CEO of Apple, Inc
- November 3
  - Francis Beckwith, American philosopher
  - Karch Kiraly, American volleyball player
- November 4 – Frl. Menke, German pop singer
- November 5 – Tilda Swinton, British actress
- November 9
  - Andreas Brehme, German football player and manager
  - Joëlle Ursull, Guadeloupean singer
- November 10 – Neil Gaiman, English author
- November 11 – Stanley Tucci, American actor and film director
- November 15 – Susanne Lothar, German actress (d. 2012)
- November 17 – Jonathan Ross, English television presenter
- November 18 – Kim Wilde, English singer and gardener
- November 19
  - Miss Elizabeth, American professional wrestling valet (d. 2003)
  - Hiroshi Naka, Japanese voice actor
  - Matt Sorum, American drummer
- November 20 – Marc Labrèche, Canadian actor and television host
- November 24 – Amanda Wyss, American actress

- November 25
  - Amy Grant, American Christian and pop musician
  - John F. Kennedy Jr., American lawyer, journalist and son of 35th President John F. Kennedy (d. 1999)
  - Kasey Smith, American keyboardist (Danger Danger)
- November 26 – Harold Reynolds, American baseball player and broadcaster
- November 27
  - Eike Immel, German football player and manager
  - Tim Pawlenty, American politician
  - Yulia Tymoshenko, Prime Minister of Ukraine
- November 30
  - Rich Fields, American television personality
  - Gary Lineker, English footballer and sports presenter

December

Daryl Hannah

Julianne Moore

Kenneth Branagh

- December 1 – Carol Alt, American model and actress
- December 2
  - Rick Savage, British rock musician (Def Leppard)
  - Sydney Youngblood, American singer
- December 3
  - Daryl Hannah, American actress
  - Julianne Moore, American actress
- December 4 – Glynis Nunn, Australian athlete
- December 5
  - Brian Bromberg, American jazz bassist and composer
  - Jack Russell, American rock singer (Great White)
- December 9
  - Steve Doll, American professional wrestler (d. 2009)
  - Jeff "Swampy" Marsh, American television director, writer, producer, storyboard artist, and actor
- December 10
  - Kenneth Branagh, Northern Irish actor and director
  - Michael Schoeffling, American actor and model
- December 12
  - Volker Beck, German politician
- December 17 – Tarako, Japanese voice actress
- December 18 – Kazuhide Uekusa, Japanese economist

- December 19
  - Jon St. John, American Actor
  - Mike Lookinland, former American actor
- December 22 – Mark Brydon, British musician (Moloko)
- December 24
  - Charles Ng – Chinese-American serial killer
  - Carol Vorderman, British television presenter
- December 27
  - Maryam d'Abo, British actress
  - Fred Hammond, African-American gospel musician
- December 28
  - Ray Bourque, Canadian ice hockey player
  - John Fitzgerald, Australian tennis player
- December 29 – Dave Pelzer, American author
- December 31
  - Steve Bruce, English footballer
  - John Allen Muhammad, African-American spree killer (d. 2009)

Date unknown

- Randi Altschul, American toy inventor

Deaths

January
Albert Camus

Beno Gutenberg

- January 1 – Margaret Sullavan, American actress (b. 1909)
- January 3 – Victor Sjöström, Swedish actor (b. 1879)
- January 4
  - Albert Camus, French writer, Nobel Prize winner (b. 1913)
  - Dudley Nichols, American screenwriter (b. 1895)
- January 5 – Donald Knight, English cricketer (b. 1894)
- January 7 – Dorothea Chambers, English tennis champion (b. 1878)
- January 9 – Elsie J. Oxenham, British children's novelist (b. 1880)
- January 10 – Arthur S. Carpender, American admiral (b. 1884)
- January 12 – Nevil Shute, English writer (b. 1899)
- January 17 – Andrew Kennaway Henderson, New Zealand illustrator, cartoonist, and pacifist (b. 1879)
- January 19 – Dadasaheb Torne, Indian filmmaker (b. 1890)

- January 24
  - Matt Moore, Irish-American actor (b. 1888)
  - Edwin Fischer, Swiss pianist and conductor (b. 1886)
  - John Miljan, American actor (b. 1892)
- January 25
  - Diana Barrymore, American stage and film actress (b. 1921)
  - Beno Gutenberg, German-American seismologist (b. 1889)
- January 27 – Osvaldo Aranha, Brazilian politician (b. 1894)
- January 28 – Zora Neale Hurston, American folklorist and author (b. 1891)
- January 30 – J. C. Kumarappa, Indian economist (b. 1892)

February

- February 2 – Swami Bharati Krishna Tirtha, Hindu teacher (b. 1884)
- February 3 – Fred Buscaglione, Italian singer and actor (b. 1921)
- February 6 – Jesse Belvin, American R&B singer (b. 1932)
- February 7 – Igor Kurchatov, Soviet physicist (b. 1903)
- February 8 – J. L. Austin, British philosopher (b. 1911)
- February 10 – Aloysius Stepinac, Croatian Catholic prelate (b. 1898)
- February 11 – Ernő Dohnányi, Hungarian conductor (b. 1877)
- February 12 – Jean-Michel Atlan, French painter (b. 1913)
- February 14 – Masatomi Kimura, Japanese admiral (b. 1891)
- February 20

- o Leonard Woolley, English archaeologist (b. 1880)
- o Adone Zoli, Italian politician, former Prime Minister (b. 1887)
- February 29
  - o Jacques Becker, French director (b. 1906)
  - o Edwina Mountbatten, Countess Mountbatten of Burma (b. 1901), last Vicereine of India
  - o Melvin Purvis, American lawman (b. 1903)
  - o Walter Yust, American encyclopedia editor (b. 1894)

March

- March 2 – Stanisław Taczak, Polish general (b. 1874)
- March 4 – Leonard Warren, American opera singer (b. 1911)
- March 9 – Jack Beattie, Irish politician (b. 1886)
- March 11 – Roy Chapman Andrews, American explorer, adventurer and naturalist (b. 1884)
- March 13 – Yosef Zvi HaLevy, Israeli rabbi and judge (b.1874)
- March 23 – Franklin Pierce Adams, American journalist (b. 1881)
- March 26 – Ian Keith, American actor (b. 1899)
- March 27
  - o Mario Talavera, Mexican songwriter (b. 1885)
  - o Gregorio Marañón, Spanish physician, scientist, historian and philosopher. (b. 1887)

April

Max von Laue

- April 1 – Tuanku Abdul Rahman ibni Almarhum Tuanku Muhammad, King of Malaysia (b. 1895)
- April 5
    - Cuthbert Burnup, English sportsman (b. 1875)
    - Peter Llewelyn Davies, namesake for Peter Pan (b. 1897)
    - Alma Kruger, American actress (b. 1868)
- April 17 – Eddie Cochran, American rock singer (b. 1938)
- April 19 – Beardsley Ruml, American economist and tax plan author (b. 1894)
- April 24
    - Max von Laue, German physicist, Nobel Prize laureate (b. 1879)
    - George Relph, English actor (b. 1888)
- April 25
    - Hope Emerson, American actress (b. 1897)
    - Amānullāh Khān, former Afghan Emir and King (b. 1892)
    - Turan Emeksiz, Turkish student killed during the demonstrations (b. 1940)

May

Georges Claude

Boris Pasternak

- May 2 – Caryl Chessman, American criminal (b. 1921)
- May 3 – Masa Niemi, Finnish actor (b. 1914)
- May 8 – J. H. C. Whitehead, British mathematician (b. 1904)
- May 11 – John D. Rockefeller Jr., American philanthropist (b. 1874)
- May 12 – Prince Aly Khan, Pakistani United Nations ambassador (b. 1911)
- May 14 – Lucrezia Bori, Spanish opera singer (b. 1887)
- May 22 – İbrahim Çallı, Turkish painter (b.1882)
- May 23 – Georges Claude, French inventor (b. 1870)
- May 24 – Avraham Arnon, Israeli educator and a recipient of the Israel Prize (b. 1887)
- May 27
  - Edward Brophy, American actor (b. 1895)

- James Montgomery Flagg, American artist and illustrator (b. 1877)
- George Zucco, English actor (b. 1886)
- May 30 – Boris Pasternak, Russian writer, Nobel Prize laureate (declined) (b. 1890)
- May 31 – Walther Funk, German Nazi politician (b. 1890)

June

- June 4
  - Józef Haller de Hallenburg, Polish general (b. 1873)
  - Lucien Littlefield, American actor (b. 1895)
- June 14 – Ana Pauker, Romanian communist politician (b. 1893)
- June 17 – Arthur Rosson, English film director (b. 1886)
- June 18 – Shalva Aleksi-Meskhishvili, Georgian politician (b. 1884)
- June 19 – Chris Bristow, English race car driver (b. 1937)
- June 20
  - William E. Fairbairn, English soldier, police officer, and hand-to-hand combat expert (b. 1885)
  - John B. Kelly, Sr., American rower, father of Grace Kelly (b. 1889)
- June 25
  - Walter Baade, German astronomer (b. 1893)
  - Otto Ender, 9th Chancellor of Austria (b. 1875)
  - Tommy Corcoran, American baseball player (b. 1869)
- June 27 – Lottie Dod, English tennis player; Wimbledon women's champion, 1887–88, 1891-93 (b. 1871)

July

- July 6 – Aneurin Bevan, Welsh politician (b. 1897)
- July 14 – Maurice, 6th duc de Broglie, French physicist (b. 1875)
- July 15
  - Anton Giulio Bragaglia, Italian cinematographer (b. 1890)
  - Set Persson, Swedish politician (b. 1897)
  - Lawrence Tibbett, American opera singer and actor (b. 1896)
- July 16
  - Albert Kesselring, German field marshal (b. 1885)
  - John P. Marquand, American novelist (b. 1893)
- July 22 – Buddy Adler, American film producer (b. 1909)
- July 24 – Hans Albers, German actor and singer (b. 1891)
- July 26 – Cedric Gibbons, Irish-American art director (b. 1893)
- July 28 – Enrique Amorim, Uruguayan novelist (b. 1900)
- July 29 – Hasan Saka, former Prime Minister of Turkey (b. 1885)

August

- August 5 – Arthur Meighen, 9th Prime Minister of Canada (b. 1874)
- August 7
  - Walden L. "Pug" Ainsworth, American admiral (b. 1886)
  - Luis Ángel Firpo, Argentine boxer (b. 1894)

- August 10
  - Frank Lloyd, American film director (b. 1886)
  - Oswald Veblen, American mathematician, geometer and topologist (b. 1880)
- August 14 – Fred Clarke, American baseball player (Pittsburgh Pirates) and a member of the MLB Hall of Fame (b. 1872)
- August 17 – Charles W. Ryder, American general (b. 1892)
- August 22
  - Eduard Pütsep, Estonian wrestler (b. 1898)
  - Johannes Sikkar, Estonian politician (b. 1897)
- August 23
  - Jersey Flegg, English-Australian rugby league player and chairman (b. 1878)
  - Oscar Hammerstein II, American librettist (b. 1895)
  - Bruno Loerzer, German aviator and air force general (b. 1891)
- August 27 – Stanley Clifford Weyman, American impostor (b. 1890)
- August 28 – Charles Forbes, British Admiral (b. 1880)
- August 29
  - Vicki Baum, Austrian writer (b. 1888)
  - David Diop, French West African poet (b. 1927)

September

- September 1 – Hisamuddin Alam Shah ibni Almarhum Sultan Alaeddin Sulaiman Shah, King of Malaysia (b. 1898)
- September 4 – Alfred E. Green, American film director (b. 1889)

- September 8
  - Feroze Gandhi, Indian politician (b. 1912)
  - Oscar Pettiford, American jazz string player (b. 1922)
- September 9 – Jussi Björling, Swedish tenor (b. 1911)
- September 11 – Edwin Justus Mayer, American screenwriter (b. 1896)
- September 13 – Leó Weiner, Hungarian composer (b. 1885)
- September 20 – Ida Rubinstein, Russian ballet dancer (b. 1885)
- September 22 – Melanie Klein, Austrian-British psychoanalyst (b. 1882)
- September 23 – Kathlyn Williams, American stage and silent film actress (b. 1879)
- September 24 – Mátyás Seiber, Hungarian composer (b. 1905)
- September 27 – Sylvia Pankhurst, English suffragette (b. 1882)
- September 30 – St John Philby, British Arabist (b. 1885)

October

- October 11 – Richard Cromwell, American actor (b. 1910)
- October 12 – Inejiro Asanuma, Japanese Socialist politician (assassinated) (b. 1898)
- October 15
  - Henny Porten, German actress (b. 1890)
  - Clara Kimball Young, American actress (b. 1890)
- October 21 – Ma Hongbin, Chinese warlord (b. 1884)
- October 24 – Yevgeny Ostashev, was the test pilot of rocket and space complexes, head of the 1st control polygon NIIP-5

(Baikonur), Lenin prize winner, Candidate of Technical Sciences, engineer-Lieutenant Colonel.(b. 1924)
- October 31 – H. L. Davis, American author (b. 1894)

November

Clark Gable

- November 2
    - Dimitri Mitropoulos, Greek conductor, pianist, and composer (b. 1896)
    - Otoya Yamaguchi ultranationalist who assassinated Inejiro Asanuma, a politician and head of the Japan Socialist Party (d. 1960)
- November 3
    - Bobby Wallace, American baseball player (St. Louis Browns) and a member of the MLB Hall of Fame (b. 1873)
    - Harold Spencer Jones, English astronomer (b. 1890)
- November 5
    - Ward Bond, American actor (b. 1903)
    - August Gailit, Estonian writer (b. 1891)
    - Johnny Horton, American country singer (b. 1925)
    - Mack Sennett, Canadian film producer and director (b. 1880)

- o Erich Neumann, German psychologist (b. 1905)
- November 6 – Erich Raeder, German World War II naval leader (b. 1876)
- November 7 – A. P. Carter, American singer and songwriter (b. 1891)
- November 12 – Lord Buckley, American monologist (b. 1906)
- November 14 – Walter Catlett, American actor (b. 1889)
- November 16
  - o Clark Gable, American actor (b. 1901)
  - o Paul Faure, French Socialist politician (b. 1878)
- November 19 – Phyllis Haver, American actress (b. 1899)
- November 20 – Ya'akov Cohen, Israeli poet (b. 1881)
- November 23 – Allen Hobbs, 32nd Governor of American Samoa (b. 1889)
- November 24 – Grand Duchess Olga Alexandrovna of Russia, sister of Tsar Nicholas II (b. 1882)
- November 25 – Patria (b. 1924), Minerva (b. 1926), and Maria Teresa Mirabal (b. 1935), three Dominican revolutionaries (and their driver, Rufino de la Cruz)
- November 28
  - o Richard Wright, American novelist (b. 1908)
  - o Dirk Jan de Geer, 30th and 33rd Prime Minister of the Netherlands (b. 1870)

December

- December 2 – Fritz August Breuhaus de Groot, German architect, interior designer and designer (b. 1883)
- December 7 – Ioannis Demestichas, Greek admiral (b. 1882)

- December 13 – John Charles Thomas, American opera singer (b. 1891)
- December 14 – Gregory Ratoff, Russian actor and director
- December 20 – Sir Godfrey Ince, British civil servant (b. 1891)
- December 26
  - Giuseppe Bellanca, Italian-American aircraft designer and company founder (b. 1886)
  - Watsuji Tetsuro, Japanese philosopher (b. 1889)

Date unknown

- Guillermo Sánchez Boix, Spanish cartoonist (b. 1917)

Nobel Prizes

- Physics – Donald Arthur Glaser
- Chemistry – Willard Libby
- Physiology or Medicine – Sir Frank Macfarlane Burnet, Peter Medawar
- Literature – Saint-John Perse
- Peace – Albert Lutuli

In the News.

Tidal Wave at Agadir in Morocco kills 12,000.

The new capital city of Brazil Brasilia is officially inaugurated on April 21, 1960.

100,000 Join "Ban The Bomb" Rally on <u>April 18th</u> in London.

John F Kennedy wins presidential Election.

The United States announces that 3,500 American soldiers are going to be sent to Vietnam.

Princess Margaret marries Antony Armstrong Jones.

The Summer Olympics are held in Rome, Italy.

Coronation Street Soap premieres on ITV in the UK.

Popular Films - Ben-Hur, Can Can, Psycho.

Aluminum Cans **used for the first time.**

Inventions - Laser and **Heart Pacemaker.**

1960 Calender.

January 1960
Sun	Mon	Tue	Wed	Thu	Fri	Sat
					1	2
3	4	5	6	7	8	9
10	11	12	13	14	15	16
17	18	19	20	21	22	23
24	25	26	27	28	29	30
31						

February 1960
Sun	Mon	Tue	Wed	Thu	Fri	Sat
	1	2	3	4	5	6
7	8	9	10	11	12	13
14	15	16	17	18	19	20
21	22	23	24	25	26	27
28	29					

March 1960
Sun	Mon	Tue	Wed	Thu	Fri	Sat
		1	2	3	4	5
6	7	8	9	10	11	12
13	14	15	16	17	18	19
20	21	22	23	24	25	26
27	28	29	30	31		

April 1960
Sun	Mon	Tue	Wed	Thu	Fri	Sat
					1	2
3	4	5	6	7	8	9
10	11	12	13	14	15	16
17	18	19	20	21	22	23
24	25	26	27	28	29	30

May 1960
Sun	Mon	Tue	Wed	Thu	Fri	Sat
1	2	3	4	5	6	7
8	9	10	11	12	13	14
15	16	17	18	19	20	21
22	23	24	25	26	27	28
29	30	31				

June 1960
Sun	Mon	Tue	Wed	Thu	Fri	Sat
			1	2	3	4
5	6	7	8	9	10	11
12	13	14	15	16	17	18
19	20	21	22	23	24	25
26	27	28	29	30		

July 1960
Sun	Mon	Tue	Wed	Thu	Fri	Sat
					1	2
3	4	5	6	7	8	9
10	11	12	13	14	15	16
17	18	19	20	21	22	23
24	25	26	27	28	29	30
31						

August 1960
Sun	Mon	Tue	Wed	Thu	Fri	Sat
	1	2	3	4	5	6
7	8	9	10	11	12	13
14	15	16	17	18	19	20
21	22	23	24	25	26	27
28	29	30	31			

September 1960
Sun	Mon	Tue	Wed	Thu	Fri	Sat
				1	2	3
4	5	6	7	8	9	10
11	12	13	14	15	16	17
18	19	20	21	22	23	24
25	26	27	28	29	30	

October 1960
Sun	Mon	Tue	Wed	Thu	Fri	Sat
						1
2	3	4	5	6	7	8
9	10	11	12	13	14	15
16	17	18	19	20	21	22
23	24	25	26	27	28	29
30	31					

November 1960
Sun	Mon	Tue	Wed	Thu	Fri	Sat
		1	2	3	4	5
6	7	8	9	10	11	12
13	14	15	16	17	18	19
20	21	22	23	24	25	26
27	28	29	30			

December 1960
Sun	Mon	Tue	Wed	Thu	Fri	Sat
				1	2	3
4	5	6	7	8	9	10
11	12	13	14	15	16	17
18	19	20	21	22	23	24
25	26	27	28	29	30	31